So
You Think
Your Family Is
Messed Up

Julie Ann Bailey

Published by BookLocker.com, Inc., St. Petersburg, Florida.

Printed on acid-free paper.

BookLocker.com, Inc.
2018

First Edition

Foreword

Rédemption.

According to Webster's dictionary this word means "an act of redeeming or atoning for a fault or mistake, deliverance, rescue, recovery by payment." This is what "So You Think Your Family Is Messed Up" is all about. Redemption.

It's a story of how a broken family produced broken children, how life piled on disappointments and even more pain and yet how all that dysfunction was turned around because someone decided "enough is enough." In that determination and reaching out to God for answers, entire families and generations could experience a better life and a more fulfilling future. It is a message of hope that no matter how bad things are a person's life, family and destiny anyone can experience this miracle of transformation, freedom and joy.

My husband Tom and I have been in ministry together for over 35 years. We have pastored a thriving church, traveled to many nations to speak and have even met with renowned leaders for prayer and personal ministry. Everywhere we go, and everyone we meet with have this in common: they have either experienced the life changing power of redemption and the blessings and benefits this brings or they are in desperate need of being redeemed. Mankind needed redemption, which is why God sent His Only Son into the earth, to turn everything around for us.

We are indeed living in an upside-down world: a time when they call good evil and evil good. Over 50% of marriages end in divorce, one third of this current generation that should have been alive today lost their lives in the travesty of abortion, 20% of the 30 and under age group are unaffiliated with any religious organization, and the church is losing 90% of people after they turn 18 years of age. The dysfunction of our society is clearly reflected in the statistics of domestic violence, child abuse, drug and alcohol abuse, sexual abuse, teen pregnancy and unwed mothers of all ages, human trafficking and suicide which are all on the rise. If ever there was a time in history when mankind needed to experience redemption it is now. But thank God that through finding healing and hope through a personal relationship with Jesus Christ, we can see what is upside down turned right side up.

I have known Greg and Julie Bailey for over 20 years. My husband and I have been in their home, watched their beautiful family grow up and thrive and have walked alongside them as God created a platform in their lives to make them a voice to the nations. They are the real deal! Out of their places of brokenness they now minister breakthrough to thousands. Out of their mess God has developed a message.

Jane Hamon, Senior Pastor, Apostle

Vision Church, Christian International

Santa Rosa Beach, Florida.

Acknowledgements

First and most importantly, thanks to my Heavenly Father who has always loved me. He has been my greatest constant. He is my faithful friend and my rock. I am forever grateful for His love and all that He has done for me.

My amazing Husband, you have loved me unconditionally from day one. This has made me a better person. You have been my greatest encourager. Your encouragement and love has pushed me to higher heights.

Cindi, Ben, Sarah, Brad, Benjamin, Dashelle, our five beautiful grandchildren Houston, BJ, Jameson, Zara and Savannah, you are the greatest gifts. We have had a hard and long fight for this generational blessing, but we see what the Lord has done and what He is doing. It is all worth it. The love that abounds in our family and the presence of God in all our lives is a testimony to God's power.

Bishop Hamon, Apostles Tom and Jane Hamon, Apostles Leon and Donna Walters, your mentoring, leadership, and the way you honour God is inspiring. Your selflessness for the Kingdom is a powerful example to all. Thank you for loving and believing in us. We honour you and love you.

Dariel Forlong, thank you for helping me put all these words together and pushing me to write this book. I finally finished it while recovering with a broken leg ☺

Caralise Trayes, thank you for your editing skills.

To all my dear friends who kept asking me "Is your book published yet?" Thank you for keeping me accountable to finish this project.

Contents

Preface

There are so many messed-up families around today. I came from one of them.

I want to share with you an honest account of my life and the pain and misery that comes from being part of a dysfunctional family. Unless we deal with our upbringing it has a marked effect on our future and destiny.

I feel God has given me insight and keys into this subject. I know through my own experience that God is able to turn a life that was doomed for destruction into one that has a wonderful future and destiny to fulfil.

When we take His hand, He changes us. Not just us, but a whole generation. Broken families produce broken children. No matter how bad things are in your life or family you can experience a miracle of transformation.

Let me take you on this journey and show from the scriptures a dysfunctional family that experienced a turnaround as God intervened in their lives.

I know that if you are in a similar situation you will find keys to bring release and freedom, keys to give you a future and hope.

Chapter One

Totally Messed-Up

Complicated, messed-up families are very common these days. Many people find themselves living in horrendous circumstances which destroy any hope of them reaching their potential and destiny. I know this reality personally as I was in one of them.

My life was complicated and full of pain, rejection, heartache and disaster because I came from a messed-up family.

The brokenness in my parents was the result of the family and circumstances they had been brought up in. My Mum and Dad became parents at age seventeen. They were far too young and broken to make family life work, and both brought their own problems into the marriage.

Sadly, I don't have any memories of my parents being together. They had a pattern of living together then separating. When I was ten years old they finally parted for good.

After my Mum left, my brother and I stayed with our Dad. We spent most of the time alone as Dad worked during the day and attended night school after work.

The weekends were also spent alone. We never saw my father from Friday until Sunday night.

It was a very sad, hard time in our lives. I remember hearing a song that described how I felt at that time. The lyrics went like this:

I'm nobody's child
I'm nobody's child
Just like the flowers
I am growing wild.
I've got no mammy's kisses
I've got no daddy's smile
Nobody wants me
I'm nobody's child.

I remember other children's parents calling them inside, but there was no one to call us in.

This is when so much of my world changed, and so many things happened that changed my life forever.

In this book I don't want to major on the details, or place blame. Most of us have had bad things happen to us. You can't change the past, but you can change the future.

This book is about how I learnt to walk in victory and how my life has changed. Because of these changes the lives of my children and children's children have changed.

Neither of my parents had any idea where they were going or what they were doing with their lives. They had no vision, no sense of purpose, and no role models to speak into them or show them how to do life well.

What we call the 'cycle of life' began from their families' brokenness and was passed onto my parents, and from my parents onto me. How can you stop this madness? How can you break the cycle?

In 1982 I made a decision that changed my life and the life of my family. This began to change what seemed inevitable. I was lifted out of the sinking sand. For me it was a cycle that God fixed and made right.

I also discovered a family of ages past which a number of people can relate to. They had their own crazy, mixed up life. But in the midst of all the hurt, betrayal and brokenness there was a turn-around, just as there was in my life.

I gained so much hope, strength and insight into how to change the inevitable spiral for me and the generations to follow.

Let us start our journey by looking at the lives of Leah and Rachel in the book of Genesis.

Genesis 29:20-25 So Jacob served seven years to get Rachel, but they seemed like only a few days to him because of his love for her. Then Jacob said to Laban, "Give me my wife. My time is completed, and I want to lie with her." So Laban brought together all the people of the place and gave a feast. But when evening came, he took his daughter Leah and gave her to Jacob, and Jacob lay with her. And Laban gave his servant girl Zilpah to his daughter as her maidservant. When morning came, there was Leah! So Jacob said to Laban, "What is this you have done to me? I served you for Rachel, didn't I? Why have you deceived me?"

Let's look at the chain of events. It was the beginning of a disaster. This whole family's life changed in one night. Oh, how one night can change so much!

One night, one event, or one action by someone else has changed many of our lives forever.

Jacob had served Laban for seven long years for Rachel to become his wife. Every day I am sure that through his toil all he thought about was Rachel. He took comfort after a hard day's work when he was with her, his beloved Rachel. They talked together of their hopes, dreams and plans. The passion grew between them and they longed for their wedding day. Now that day finally arrived.

Jacob does not hold back, he wants her as his wife, so he can be one with Rachel in every way. His passion and desire is burning within him. After all, he is a red-hot blooded young man and he has waited seven years for this day.

Rachel is thinking about her 'knight in shining armour' who has worked so hard for her and is now going to make her life complete. She has dreamed of this day. She knows what she will wear. Every detail is covered even down to the perfume to be used. Rachel has thought about the endless, romantic candlelight nights under the stars with her beloved Jacob. She has envisaged the children they will have together and the life they will live.

The wedding feast is set in place and all the people gather to celebrate the event. Jacob was so besotted by his burning desire to sleep with Rachel he does not notice a devastating deception has taken place, a deception that will affect his life forever.

Interesting – if we take a look back into Jacob's earlier life we see that Jacob was known as the deceiver. Jacob stole his elder brother's birthright by deception. Could this be Jacob reaping from the deception earlier in his life? The deception of this day begins a life of misery and destruction for this family.

Not only do we have a bridegroom who has been deceived, but we have a father who has now set his daughters up to a life of competition and jealousy between them.

These sisters were probably very close before this incident came to ruin their lives. They would have discussed their future plans, hopes and dreams for their lives, their future husbands, weddings, and the children that would come from these unions.

The lives of these two girls would never be the same again. Leah is dealt a double blow. Not only is she living with a man who does not love her but she also has to live with a sister who despises her.

It must have been the lowest point of her life. Everything that was done this day was not her choice. She was not consulted about what she would like, she had no choice but to do what she was told. Her future and destiny were now a foregone conclusion.

Leah would have felt very lonely and unloved with no way of escape. She had lost so much that day. She did not ask for it, and certainly did not deserve it.

All Leah wanted was what everyone wants, someone who would love and cherish her, someone who would respect her and the qualities she would bring to marriage.

For so many of us today our future gets chosen through circumstances or incidents at the hands of others. Many of us are too young to know why or how everything suddenly changed. In reality it has, and how do we deal with that? Life will never be the same again.

Just like Leah, I had a desire for someone to love and cherish me. I had a dream like most little girls do of 'Prince Charming' coming on his white horse sweeping me away to live happily ever after.

What is it with all those Disney movies where Prince Charming comes and rescues the princess and they live happily ever after? The reality is that most of us never get to experience this fairy-tale without God in our lives. Statistics are so high of both male and females being sexually abused, either by family members, or by someone close to them.

I was one of those statistics! When abuse or rape happens you feel unclean, used like second-hand goods, worth nothing. You ask the question, "Did I do something to attract this? Maybe I deserved it?" Your whole perspective of love changes along with perspective of yourself. You have been robbed of your purity, your gift to the man who would be your future husband.

Suddenly your dreams turn into a nightmare. All your innocence, security and dreams are gone in an instant. You ask yourself, "Will I ever feel the same again?"

Life suddenly changes forever and things become a blur. You feel alone, even in a crowded room. You want to scream and tell someone what has happened to you, but who would believe you?

You feel so unclean and do not want anyone else to see your uncleanness, so you keep it all inside and get on with life hoping that one day you will wake up and find it was all a bad dream.

Leah had all her dreams taken from her the night her father made her go into the wedding chambers with Jacob. Imagine the feelings that would have overwhelmed her. This was not how she had envisaged her wedding night to be. She knew from that moment on she would always be second choice to Rachel. Imagine how that made her feel.

What a horrible night that must have been for her, knowing that at some point Jacob would realise it was her, not Rachel he had spent his wedding night with. Imagine the rejection she would have felt when Jacob said to her father, "What have you done to me?"

Leah would have felt worthless, lonely and abandoned. She and Jacob would have to complete and fulfil their bridal week. I am sure that this bridal week would have been shattering for Leah knowing that Jacob only had love for Rachel.

Leah, like all of us who have been a victim, could never imagine how something so beautiful could go so horribly wrong. BUT God had a plan for Leah, just as He has for each one of us.

Chapter Two

God Has a Purpose for Us

I believe that Leah could not see any purpose for her life at this point. That's how I felt. You too may also be at this place.

She was hurt, confused, rejected and unloved.

But God had a plan for Leah just like He has a plan for each one of us.

Genesis 29:31-35 When the LORD saw that Leah was not loved, he opened her womb, but Rachel was barren. Leah became pregnant and gave birth to a son. She named him Reuben, for she said, "It is because the LORD has seen my misery. Surely my husband will love me now." She conceived again, and when she gave birth to a son she said, "Because the LORD heard that I am not loved, he gave me this one too." So, she named him Simeon. Again she conceived, and when she gave birth to a son she said, "Now at last my husband will become attached to me, because I have borne him three sons." So he was named Levi. She conceived again, and when she gave birth to a son she said, "This time I will praise the LORD." So she named him Judah. Then she stopped having children.

God saw the pain, rejection and heartache and knew that Leah was unloved, so He blessed her with children.

Like all of us Leah was yearning to be loved and cherished. She had the mindset that "If I produce a son, then my husband will love me". This is not the way love should work. We should be loved for who we are, not what we can do.

All through this scripture you can hear her heartfelt cry, "now my husband will love me". But still Jacob loved Rachel more than anyone else.

So many young girls think like Leah. "If I sleep with this guy then he will love me", or "If I do that for him, he will have to care for me". I used to think the same. When you are lonely and looking for love and security anything someone says to you that sounds even slightly like love is appealing.

Guys told me how much they loved me and said all the right words that I longed to hear just so I would sleep with them. Once they had their way with me I was discarded and despised. This left me even more empty and confused. "Last night was so different with accolades of love and concern, but today there is just rejection and that deep loneliness that eats away at me".

The hurt and rejection keeps going deeper until you begin to hate yourself and wonder what is wrong with you. "Why doesn't anybody love me?" With each rejection, the longing to be loved and cared for becomes stronger and stronger. "Surely, somewhere there is a man that wants to love me and be loved in return. Somewhere there must be a man that can give me the care and protection that I yearn for."

Time and again we fall into the same trap, "Surely this is the one who will love me". We were created to be loved and we become so desperate that we settle for whatever comes our way, not taking into account the incredible toll it takes on us in every area of life.

It was not until Leah had given birth to her fourth son that she finally turns to God. There was nothing Leah could do to change the circumstances of her life. She couldn't make Jacob love her.

Genesis 29:35 She conceived again, and when she gave birth to a son she said, "This time I will praise the LORD." So she named him Judah. Then she stopped having children.

I believe Leah knew about God, but perhaps did not know Him as her Saviour or her heavenly Father. It seems she did not know how to totally surrender her life to Him. Once she did, she realised that God had a plan for her.

After giving birth to her fourth son Judah (his name means praise), she begins to see God as her source. Her life takes on a brand new perspective. Instead of complaining about her circumstances, being miserable and depressed, she realises that only God can bring her the fulfilment, wholeness and happiness.

Once Leah took her focus off what she didn't have and began to thank God for what she did have she became a different person with a different outlook on life.

Genesis 30:13 "I am happy, for the daughters will call me blessed." NKJV

After she turned her mess over to God and praised Him, she could say 'I am happy and I will be called blessed'. I believe this was a turnaround for her.

Was life perfect? No, certainly not, and in the natural nothing had changed. But Leah now had an inner peace that came from God. Being happy does not mean everything is perfect, but rather you decide to look beyond the imperfections. I believe she was making a statement, 'I will be called blessed'. Half of the battle in our lives comes from our belief system. If you believe you are unhappy, then that is what you will be. If you believe you are a victim, then you will always be a victim.

I always believed my life would get better. I knew I was going to make it. I was not going to allow my past to dictate my future.

Chapter Three

Rising Above, Being Unloved

In my own life this pattern continued. I was not only abused but raped by a friend of someone I knew. At 4am I was dumped on the streets a long way from home. I was just 15 years old. This was the worst, most frightening thing that had ever happened to me in my short life.

I felt so filthy, unloved and unworthy. For the next few months my life was a daze. I was desperate. I cried so much and wondered if anybody would ever love me. I just wanted to go to sleep, wake up and believe it was just a bad dream and that it would all go away.

I was living with one of Mum's friends. They really didn't want me but felt obliged as I did not have anywhere else to live. My mother remarried and had moved to another state. At this point we didn't have an open relationship with each other. My mother was an orphan and never knew her parents.

My father was in the midst of a nervous breakdown. My grandparents on my father's side died before I was born.

I didn't have any really close friends at this point in my life. When you live in a dysfunctional family you are often awkward and dysfunctional yourself and don't know how to form close friendships or connect with people. I was forced to become an adult at a young age. I had to grow up fast but without any nurturing or role models how do you learn what is normal and what isn't?

I had no one I could talk to and felt that everything was my fault entirely. I deserved what had happened to me. I was learning the hard lessons in life very quickly.

Somewhere, deep inside of me I found a strength that I now believe was the Spirit of God, even though at this point I did not know Him personally. I knew there was a God out there somewhere and I would always pray the Lord's Prayer every night. That was my total knowledge of God.

I believe God was with me at this point, the lowest in my life. It was right then and there that I made a decision that I was not going to become a victim of what had happened to me. I knew this was not love, and I was not going to find love or acceptance by sleeping with someone. None of these guys cared for me or about me. I was someone they could take advantage of. But not anymore, my life was going to change. My life was going to matter and no one would ever do this to me again.

Even though I didn't know God the way I know Him today, He knew me and He had wonderful plans for my life.

Jeremiah 29:11-13 "For I know the plans I have for you," declares the LORD, "plans to prosper you and not to harm you, plans to give you hope and a future. Then you will call upon me and come and pray to me, and I will listen to you. You will seek me and find me when you seek me with all your heart..."

God had plans for me to prosper. He had a future and a hope for me. God was waiting for me to find Him and put my life into His wonderful loving hands. He was just waiting for me to seek Him, but God was there even though I didn't know Him!

Jeremiah 1:5 "Before I formed you in the womb I knew you, before you were born I set you apart..."

God knew me before I was formed in my mother's womb. He planned every day of my life before I even took my first breath. He set life before me and He was waiting for me to choose the life He had for me.

I often wondered why God just didn't make us all love Him and choose Him. That to me would have been much easier. He later revealed to me that love that is forced on us is not perfect love. Would I want a husband to tell me every day like a robot that he loved me because he had to? Of course I wouldn't. God doesn't want to force us to love Him. He wants us to choose Him freely and love Him because we want to love Him.

When Leah decided to rise above her feelings of being unloved and choose God it was then she could say "Now I am happy". But her life and her family were not yet whole and healed.

Chapter Four

So You Think Your Family Is Messed Up?

Leah and her family were incredibly messed up. There was rejection and hurt, one sister was raped, the sons were murderers, and so the list goes on. I wonder if this sounds anything like your family or a family you know. This could be any number of families living in our society today.

Let's take a closer look at this story.

We have two wives, step-brothers and sisters all living in the same household. To make matters even worse, the father only loves one of his wives and favours one son more than the others. The scene is set for disaster.

Poor Jacob. He is adding fuel to an already difficult situation. His family is already stressed and filled with tension. However, Jacob did not choose his life. He only ever loved Rachel. She was the one he worked seven years for to secure marriage. But he was tricked and then had to deal with another wife, Leah.

This whole situation brought tension and jealousy between Leah and Rachel, along with hurt and disappointment because of Rachel's initial inability to have children.

It seems that Jacob is also in a mess because he didn't have the capacity to deal with the problems emotionally. Therefore, he treats his son Joseph that was born from the woman he loved with more love and favour than Leah's sons.

Jacob has now created a whole generation of children that are unloved, rejected, and full of hate and jealousy.

Why were they and their mother unloved and rejected? What had they done to deserve this treatment at the hands of Jacob?

Once again, we see that they just wanted love and acceptance. I am sure they could not understand why Jacob loved Rachel and Joseph more than their mother and siblings.

Genesis 37:3-4 Now Israel loved Joseph more than any of his other sons, because he had been born to him in his old age; and he made a richly ornamented robe for him. When his brothers saw that their father loved him more than any of them, they hated him and could not speak a kind word to him.

Jacob does not try to hide the fact that Joseph is his favoured son. To rub salt into an already gaping wound, he makes Joseph a richly ornamented robe. What was he thinking?

I can't help but feel that James Dobson's books on parenting would have been a great help to Jacob right at this point. Jacob would have done well to read them. Everyone knows that it is detrimental to all the family if a parent favours one child above the other children.

Jacob has caused a big problem in his family and the gap between the children only got bigger as the days went by. The boys watched their mother being rejected and unloved and now this rejection and lack of relationship with their father was affecting them directly. Why didn't their father love them like he loved Rachel and Joseph? What had they done to deserve this sort of treatment from their father?

The results of this were very apparent. They hated Joseph and could not speak a kind word to him.

I wonder what Joseph was thinking? It seems from what we know of his early life that he was oblivious to the extra treatment he was getting from his father. He was obviously so bold and confident in his future and who he was that he didn't appear to consider or know the jealousy his brothers had towards him.

One thing Joseph seemed to lack in his life was wisdom. He reveals a dream about his greatness and this was the last straw for his brothers.

Let us read how a lack of wisdom can cause ultimate pain in our lives as it certainly did in the life of Joseph.

Genesis 37:10-11 When he told his father as well as his brothers, his father rebuked him and said, "What is this dream you had? Will your mother and I and your brothers actually come and bow down to the ground before you?" His brothers were jealous of him, but his father kept the matter in mind.

The difference between Joseph and his brothers is very evident in these verses. It was all because he was the loved and favoured son. Joseph's confidence and security in his future were so evident, but his brothers showed no such confidence in any area of their lives.

I believe Jacob had also taught Joseph about the ways of God and because of his close relationship with his father it was so much easier for him to accept and know God as his heavenly Father.

How different he was. He grew up loved and affirmed. He also had a dream and vision for his life. It was this dream that kept Joseph through the times of rejection, slavery, and his time as a prisoner.

There is power in knowing your God-given dream and purpose in life.

His brothers had no God-given dreams. They were without vision and purpose for their lives. This was a difficult life for them, it seemed so unfair in comparison to the life Joseph had.

It is interesting to notice that Joseph went from strength to strength and never harboured any hatred towards his brothers, even after what they did to him. Right to the end of his life he never blamed his brothers. Joseph knew God and His purpose.

Genesis 45:4-8 Then Joseph said to his brothers, "Come close to me." When they had done so, he said, "I am your brother Joseph, the one you sold into Egypt! And now, do not be distressed and do not be angry with yourselves for selling me here, because it was to save lives that God sent me ahead of you. For two years now there has been famine in the land, and for the next five years there will be no ploughing and reaping. But God sent me ahead of you to preserve for you a remnant on earth and to save your lives by a great deliverance.

"So then, it was not you who sent me here, but God. He made me father to Pharaoh, lord of his entire household and ruler of all Egypt.

His brothers on the other hand allowed their hatred for Joseph to intensify to such a degree that they plotted to kill him.

Genesis 37:19-20 "Here comes that dreamer!" they said to each other. "Come now, let's kill him and throw him into one of these cisterns and say that a ferocious animal devoured him. Then we'll see what comes of his dreams."

When you grow up in a family unloved, not affirmed, with no dream or purpose, it affects you and your whole outlook on life.

Rejection caused them to hate Joseph. He was to them the source of all their pain. It seemed easier just to be rid of him and his dreams, but little did they know how much pain this would cause them all.

Rejection can cause such division, jealousy and hatred in our lives towards people who are confident and successful. Perhaps you have grown up in a family where one was always favoured and loved over you. They succeed in all they do. You on the other hand feel like you can never do anything right. You have spent your life trying to measure up, but nothing you do is ever enough.

This was the point Joseph's brothers had come to, but revenge and hatred was not the answer. It only made things worse.

Chapter Five

Unresolved Issues Never Go Away

Unresolved issues in our lives must be dealt with otherwise our ultimate destiny is in jeopardy. It's interesting that Judah, the son that changed Leah's life, is the one who stepped in and stopped his brothers from killing Joseph.

Genesis 37:26-28 Judah said to his brothers, "What will we gain if we kill our brother and cover up his blood? Come, let's sell him to the Ishmaelites and not lay our hands on him, after all, he is our brother, our own flesh and blood." His brothers agreed. So when the Midianite merchants came by, his brothers pulled Joseph up out of the cistern and sold him for twenty shekels of silver to the Ishmaelites, who took him to Egypt.

The brothers thought they had got rid of the source of all their problems, but it just got worse. The seed of unresolved issues, hatred and jealousy starts to grow and reproduce in their lives. It becomes a web of lies, deceit and treachery. Joseph's brothers must come up with a story to tell their father. Getting rid of Joseph has only made their problems worse. Now they must come to terms and live with the decisions and choices they have made.

Lies, death, sin and secrets. Can you even start to imagine the guilt they are feeling when they see their father in so much pain and grief, refusing to be comforted?

If they thought their father would turn to them and pour his love and affection on them they were sadly deluded. Their father is in so much pain, he will mourn Joseph until the day he dies. This household now has an added burden to bear, a father who lives in constant sadness and grief.

Genesis 37:31-35 Then they got Joseph's robe, slaughtered a goat and dipped the robe in the blood. They took the ornate robe back to their father and said, "We found this. Examine it to see whether it is your son's robe."

He recognised it and said, "It is my son's robe! Some ferocious animal has devoured him. Joseph has surely been torn to pieces."

Then Jacob tore his clothes, put on sackcloth and mourned for his son many days. All his sons and daughters came to comfort him, but he refused to be comforted. "No," he said, "I will continue to mourn until I join my son in the grave." So his father wept for him.

I am sure the brothers would have all been wondering if Joseph was dead or alive?

At any stage one of them could have confessed, but they chose not to and covered their sin. Because of their decision their lives never prospered.

Proverbs 28:13 He who conceals his sins does not prosper, but whoever confesses and renounces them finds mercy.

Covering our feelings or taking matters into our own hands only leads to more misery and destruction. Hurt people will always hurt other people. I don't believe it is intentional for most of us, it is self-preservation. Where we were once open and loving we become tough out of fear of rejection and being hurt. We don't allow ourselves to let people into our lives; hurting people and shutting them out before they can hurt us. We become sceptical of everyone's motives, and often become so self-reliant that no one can help or get through to us.

I know in my own life I lost a lot of trust in people because I was determined that no one would ever take advantage of me again. I became so self-reliant that it was hard for anyone to get near me. Many people in this situation become workaholics and spend their lives striving to be successful. It is an 'I will show them' attitude. In the process their personal life suffers. Many of these people are in and out of relationships and marriages. I have met many highly successful people in the corporate world whose lives are a mess. The mess then spirals into their families.

Others bury it, ignore it, or move away hoping it will disappear. We all have different ways of dealing with this. Unfortunately, some self-destruct or turn to substance abuse to numb the pain and dull the memories.

Let us now follow Judah's life for a while and see what becomes of him and how he handles what happened.

I believe Judah was having great difficulty living in the same house as his father. Every day of his life he saw his father living with grief and pain, knowing that he and his brothers were the source of it. He would also be living under the constant fear of his father finding out the truth.

Judah's solution to the problem is to run away and hide. He leaves home and marries a Canaanite woman. The consequence of this choice was that he turned away from following God's laws and purposes for his life.

Many people think that getting away from it all will help. Buying the house in the country, having a 'sea change', anything to stop having to face reality is the answer. But let me tell you, the pain goes everywhere you go. Only surrendering your life to God will make us whole.

Judah chose to do it his way and as we will see, the sons born to him are wicked and die.

Genesis 38:1-6 At that time, Judah left his brothers and went down to stay with a man of Adullam named Hirah. There Judah met the daughter of a Canaanite man named Shua. He married her and lay with her; she became pregnant and gave birth to a son, who was named Er. She conceived again and gave birth to a son and named him Onan. She gave birth to still another son and named him Shelah. It was at Kezib that she gave birth to him. Judah got a wife for Er, his firstborn, and her name was Tamar. NIV

Genesis 38:7-11 But Er, Judah's firstborn, was wicked in the LORD's sight; so the LORD put him to death. Then Judah said to Onan, "Lie with your brother's wife and fulfil your duty to her as a brother-in-law to produce offspring for your brother." But Onan knew that the offspring would not be his, so whenever he lay with his brother's wife, he spilled his semen on the ground to keep from producing offspring for his brother. What he did was wicked in the LORD's sight; so he put him to death also. Judah then said to his daughter-in-law Tamar, "Live as a widow in your father's house until my son Shelah grows up." For he thought, "He may die too, just like his brothers." So, Tamar went to live in her father's house. NIV

You can see how living a life without God is so destructive. Judah rejected God and His ways for his life. He became self-reliant. As the evil and destruction becomes evident and starts to grow, we see Judah living with even more pain and misery which began from being unloved by his father.

Judah's life is now the result of unresolved grief not being dealt with in his earlier years.

Chapter Six

Redemption and Turnaround

Tamar is the first person to step up and break the negative cycle in her life and in the life of Judah. She was not going to be robbed of her destiny and future at the hands of her father.

Judah's life had not turned out well. He left one set of problems only to be faced with another. In his rebellion he mixes with the wrong crowd and marries a woman that was contrary to his family's customs and beliefs.

Judah was young when his first son was born. His sons were also young when they married, and they died young. At such a young age Judah was dealing with so much.

Many young people are drawn into marriages and relationships by keeping bad company and growing familiar with the wrong people. This has a harmful effect on them and their families. The lifestyle is totally contrary to their upbringing and family's beliefs.

Judah was living with the consequences of his choices but he still did not acknowledge or see it. Instead he believes that the loss of his two sons was Tamar's fault and now he fears losing his only remaining son. Judah just wanted the problem to go away. He sends Tamar away not realising that this girl is the key to his breakthrough, and eventually the breakthrough for his family.

Sometimes is seems easier just to send the pain and the heartache away. But God wants us to be whole and to walk into our destiny, even if facing things is hard.

Judah had no intention of giving his other son to Tamar. This meant that Tamar would have been left with nothing, no honour and no income.

Tamar had tenacity. She was proactive and was not going to sit around blaming others or become a victim of the situation. While Tamar had been dealt an unfair blow she was determined not to allow it to ruin her life. Instead of dwelling on her past Tamar looked to her future and considered how she could change it. Tamar was strong and a great example of an overcomer. I am not suggesting that we resort to the measure that Tamar did. Times were different then and what Tamar did was according to the times in which she lived.

Genesis 38:12-23 After a long time Judah's wife, the daughter of Shua, died. When Judah had recovered from his grief, he went up to Timnah, to the men who were shearing his sheep, and his friend Hirah the Adullamite went with him.

When Tamar was told, "Your father-in-law is on his way to Timnah to shear his sheep,"ᴬ she took off her widow's clothes, covered herself with a veil to disguise herself, and then sat down at the entrance to Enaim, which is on the road to Timnah. For she saw that, though Shelah had now grown up, she had not been given to him as his wife.

When Judah saw her, he thought she was a prostitute, for she had covered her face. Not realising that she was his daughter-in-law, he went over to her by the roadside and said, "Come now, let me sleep with you."

"And what will you give me to sleep with you?" she asked.

"I'll send you a young goat from my flock," he said.

"Will you give me something as a pledge until you send it?" she asked.

He said, "What pledge should I give you?"

"Your seal and its cord, and the staff in your hand," she answered. So he gave them to her and slept with her, and she became pregnant by him. After she left, she took off her veil and put on her widow's clothes again.

Meanwhile Judah sent the young goat by his friend the Adullamite in order to get his pledge back from the woman, but he did not find her. He asked the men who *lived there, "Where is the shrine prostitute who was beside the road at Enaim?"*

"There hasn't been any shrine prostitute here," they said.

So he went back to Judah and said, "I didn't find her. Besides, the men who lived there said, 'There hasn't been any shrine prostitute here.'"

Then Judah said, "Let her keep what she has, or we will become a laughingstock. After all, I did send her this young goat, but you didn't find her."

Judah is still looking for opportunity to get rid of what he perceives as the problem. Through Tamar's actions he sees the error of his ways.

Genesis 38:24 -30 About three months later Judah was told, "Your daughter-in-law Tamar is guilty of prostitution, and as a result she is now pregnant." Judah said, "Bring her out and have her burned to death!" As she was being brought out, she sent a message to her father-in-law. "I am pregnant by the man who owns these," she said. And she added, "See if you recognise whose seal and cord and staff these are. "Judah recognised them and said, "She is more righteous than I, since I wouldn't give her to my son Shelah." And he did not sleep with her again.

When the time came for her to give birth, there were twin boys in her womb. As she was giving birth, one of them put out his hand; so the midwife took a scarlet thread and tied it on his wrist and said, "This one came out first." But when he drew back his hand, his brother came out, and she said, "So this is how you have broken out!" And he was named Perez. Then his brother, who had the scarlet thread on his wrist, came out and he was given the name Zerah.

God blesses Tamar and her redemption comes. Not only does God bless her but she receives a double blessing with the birth of her twins and Perez becomes the bloodline to Jesus.

We read about this in the book of Ruth. We see from these scriptures that Perez is in the royal blood line to Jesus.

Ruth 4:12, 18 Through the offspring the LORD gives you by this young woman, may your family be like that of Perez, whom Tamar bore to Judah." This, then, is the family line of Perez: Perez was the father of Hezron.

The actions of Tamar also turned Judah's heart. He is a changed man. Tamar was faced with a life of poverty and no honour until God stepped into the situation. I believe He saw the 'lion heart' in Tamar and blessed her to the extent that she was spoken about in the book of Ruth. I also believe her actions turned Judah's life around, so he could see the state of his heart and the abundant unrighteousness in his life.

Judah returns to his father's house to face the past and reconcile with God and his father. He became a leader in his family.

This was the beginning of redemption and a turnaround for Judah and his family. God was now going to bring Judah face to face with his past and the brother he had forsaken.

Chapter Seven

Family Restored and Blessed

Joseph was a man who loved God. He had done nothing wrong. It was not his fault that his father Jacob loved him and his mother more than the other siblings. Because of Jacob's love for him he was cast out and left for dead by his brothers. His life was far from easy. Joseph lived the life of a slave.

God was with Joseph and he prospered even in prison. He always kept his heart right with God even when he did not understand God was preparing him for the future. I am sure Joseph felt ripped off, forgotten and unloved, especially as he had helped others get released from prison. It was all part of God's plan, and His timing. God's timing for our lives is so important.

We can find ourselves in this same situation. We help people and see others released from their situation, but for us it seems we have been left behind and forgotten. Nothing changes.

Could you imagine what might have happened if the cup-bearer had remembered Joseph and helped get him released? Joseph would have been just another ex-prisoner with nothing to offer his family in the years of drought. They would have all perished.

God had a higher plan for Joseph, but it was to be in His timing. Sometimes we want our own situation to change and we don't understand what is happening or why. But God sees the bigger picture in 5, 10, 30, or 50 years from now. He looks and thinks generationally. We want everything here and now. He knows the right time for our redemption, just as He did with Joseph.

It was a long, hard journey from the day Joseph was thrown in the pit. But when the time was right, in just one day he went from the prison to the palace. This was his time. Joseph was the second most powerful man in the land. So much had been restored to him. Riches, honour, and now God was going to restore his family.

Genesis 42:6-9 Now Joseph was the governor of the land, the one who sold grain to all its people. So when Joseph's brothers arrived, they bowed down to him with their faces to the ground. As soon as Joseph saw his brothers, he recognised them, but he pretended to be a stranger and spoke harshly to them. "Where do you come from?" he asked. "From the land of Canaan," they replied, "to buy food." Although Joseph recognised his brothers, they did not recognise him. Then he remembered his dreams about them and said to them, "You are spies! You have come to see where our land is unprotected."

Genesis 42:18-22 On the third day, Joseph said to them, "Do this and you will live, for I fear God: If you are honest men, let one of your brothers stay here in prison, while the rest of you go and take grain back for your starving households. But you must bring your youngest brother to me, so that your words may be verified and that you may not die." This they proceeded to do. They said to one another, "Surely we are being punished because of our brother. We saw how distressed he was when he pleaded with us for his life, but we would not listen; that's why this distress has come upon us." Reuben replied, "Didn't I tell you not to sin against the boy? But you wouldn't listen! Now we must give an accounting for his blood." They did not realise that Joseph could understand them, since he was using an interpreter.

At last we see Joseph's dream coming to pass and the accusations start to flow. Each brother accused the other of the wrong they had done to Joseph. They now realise there is a consequence for sin. Their sin has caught up with them and they have to give an account for it. Joseph is testing them, he wants to know if they have changed and if they are honest men. Maybe the test came by Joseph asking for Benjamin. He wanted to see if they would forsake Benjamin just like they did to him in order to save themselves.

Jacob now has to pay a price and willingly let go of Benjamin and trust God in order for his family to live.

Jacob was still struggling to trust God. The more he hung onto the ones he loved, the more he lost. Jacob already lost Rachel and Joseph, and now the unthinkable was about to happen, he could lose Benjamin.

At first he seemed unwilling to pay the price, but eventually he gives in and sends Benjamin with his brothers to Egypt.

Genesis 42:38 But Jacob said, "My son will not go down there with you; his brother is dead and he is the only one left. If harm comes to him on the journey you are taking, you will bring my grey head down to the grave in sorrow."

It is interesting that as Jacob allows Benjamin to go down to Egypt. Even though he still has other sons alive and well he declares that Joseph is dead and that Benjamin is the only one left. It is amazing what unresolved grief can do to a person.

This would also have been hurtful for the brothers. Jacob had been wrong in favouring and loving his two sons from Rachel over Leah's sons. It was an example of extremely bad parenting and did not help the jealousy and rivalry between the boys. Little did Jacob know or understand that by letting go of Benjamin it would release and restore his family back to him.

Judah now steps up to his responsibilities as a changed man and is willing to be the guarantor for Benjamin's safety. He was prepared to take the blame for this for the rest of his life if Benjamin was not returned safely to his father.

Genesis 43:8 -9 Then Judah said to Israel his father, "Send the boy along with me and we will go at once, so that we and you and our children may live and not die. I myself will guarantee his safety, you can hold me personally responsible for him. If I do not bring him back to you and set him here before you, I will bear the blame before you all my life."

We see here that when one person stands in the gap for a family, it begins to bring redemption, forgiveness and healing of past failures. It was a test for all of them.

It was the beginning of the healing God wanted to bring to the family. Jacob had to let go of his son, the most precious thing he had, and trust God.

Joseph prepares a feast for them and blesses them, but prepares a test to see what they will do. He has a silver cup put into Benjamin's sack. Would the brothers leave Benjamin to die and make up another lie, or had they changed? It was a test from Joseph to see if his brother's hearts had changed, or were they still the same angry, jealous brothers having no concern for Benjamin or their father.

The final test. Would Judah stand up, and honour his word to his father?

Genesis 44:17-20, 33, 34 But Joseph said, "Far be it from me to do such a thing! Only the man who was found to have the cup will become my slave. The rest of you, go back to your father in peace." Then Judah went up to him and said: "Please, my lord, let your servant speak a word to my lord. Do not be angry with your servant, though you are equal to Pharaoh Himself. My lord asked his servants, 'Do you have a father or a brother?' And we answered, 'We have an aged father, and there is a young son born to him in his old age. His brother is dead, and he is the only one of his mother's sons left, and his father loves him.' "Now then, please let your servant remain here as my lord's slave in place of the boy, and let the boy return with his brothers. How can I go back to my father if the boy is not with me? No! Do not let me see the misery that would come upon my father."

Judah was good to his word. He stood a changed man and this time he was not about to make the same mistake, he was not going to let his brother die. In a complete turnaround he was willing to give himself in the place of Benjamin. He dearly loved his father and did not want to see him suffer anymore grief, knowing that he and his brothers were the total cause of his grief.

Joseph reveals his true identity.

Genesis 45:4-11 Then Joseph said to his brothers, "Come close to me." When they had done so, he said, "I am your brother Joseph, the one you sold into Egypt! And now, do not be distressed and do not be angry with yourselves for selling me here, because it was to save lives that God sent me ahead of you. For two years now there has been famine in the land, and for the next five years there will not be ploughing and reaping. But God sent me ahead of you to preserve for you a remnant on earth and to save your lives by a great deliverance. "So then, it was not you who sent me here, but God. He made me father to Pharaoh, lord of his entire household and ruler of all Egypt. Now hurry back to my father and say to him, 'This is what your son Joseph says: God has made me lord of all Egypt. Come down to me; don't delay. You shall live in the region of Goshen and be near me— you, your children and grandchildren, your flocks and herds, and all you have. I will provide for you there, because five years of famine are still to come. Otherwise you and your household and all who belong to you will become destitute."

God's plan is complete. Joseph's dream has come to pass and his family has been restored. This was one messed up family but despite how broken and impossible it was, God brought restoration.

We see as God's plan is complete He not only blesses Jacob and His family, but his children, and his grandchildren.

"You shall live in the region of Goshen and be near me— you, your children and grandchildren." Gen 45:10

It was turnaround as only God can do.

As we look back over this family's story we see through the generations all the mistakes, but we also see that after breaking the cycle they will now be blessed.

- Jacob is a deceiver and stole his brother's birthright
- His father-in-law is also a deceiver and gives him Leah, but he loves Rachel – now we have double trouble
- Leah is unloved and realises her worth is not in whether Jacob loves her
- Leah produces the son that is the seed of David and Jesus
- Leah gets to be Jacob's only wife and is buried with him and his father
- Rachel is barren, full of jealousy and stole from her father. She has two sons and dies giving birth to the second
- Rachel is buried elsewhere
- Jacob loves and favours his sons from Rachel, the other sons feel rejected and unloved

- Brothers plot to kill Joseph, but God has a purpose and a plan for the family
- Judah runs away from the problems and marries a Canaanite woman
- Two of his evil sons wrong Tamar and die
- Tamar makes good and God blesses her with twins
- Perez is in the family line of Jesus
- Judah goes back home to where it all began, a changed man and now taking responsibility in leading the family
- Judah Recognises God and willingly offers himself for his brother
- God saves the family from death through Joseph and restores them and their finances. They now have the best of the land
- Judah receives the greatest blessing from his father when he dies.

God has a plan for every person and family. We see how He turned one messed-up family around and made it good. He did it for them, He did it for me, and He will do it for you.

Chapter Eight

Restoration and Rejoicing

Family life can be a mess when we try and do it 'our way'. Circumstances and 'stuff' can make us full of jealousy, hate and evil. God had a plan for Jacob's family and it came to pass once they got their lives right and did it God's way. There was so much pain and suffering as a result of bad choices and rebellion. Doing it God's way is so much better.

When someone steps up in a family and decides to turn to God the impact is amazing. The news of this family being reunited and restored reached the King's Palace and Pharaoh was excited for Joseph, now their breakthrough was having a kingdom affect.

Genesis 45:16-24 When the news reached Pharaoh's palace that Joseph's brothers had come, Pharaoh and all his officials were pleased. Pharaoh said to Joseph, "Tell your brothers, 'Do this: Load your animals and return to the land of Canaan, and bring your father and your families back to me. I will give you the best of the land of Egypt and you can enjoy the fat of the land.' "You are also directed to tell them, 'Do this: Take some carts from Egypt for your children and your wives, and get your father and come. Never mind about your belongings, because the best of all Egypt will be yours.'" So the sons of Israel did this. Joseph gave them carts, as Pharaoh had commanded, and he also gave them provisions for their journey. To each of them he gave new clothing, but to Benjamin he gave three hundred shekels of silver and five sets of clothes. And this is what he sent to his father: ten donkeys loaded with the best things of Egypt, and ten female donkeys loaded with grain and bread and other provisions for his journey. Then he sent his brothers away, and as they were leaving he said to them, "Don't quarrel on the way!"

The news reaches Pharaoh and everyone is pleased. Joseph is to be united with his family. Pharaoh sends them back to their father loaded with gifts and a promise for them to have the best of the land.

When God brings breakthrough in our lives He restores all and does way beyond what we could ever ask, think or dream. I know He has done this in my life and the life of my family. He is faithful, He has a plan for us all, and He will do it for you and your generation as well.

The restoration of the family that day was amazing. They were at a point of facing death with no food or water. Jacob had lost one son and now had to face the possibility of losing Benjamin. But now their circumstances changed. They have the best of everything, the best land in Egypt, and the family restored. Joseph offered words of wisdom to his brothers, "don't quarrel".

Joseph had a parting message for his brothers – "don't worry about who did what to me". In other words, he was saying don't worry about the past. Joseph had already forgiven his brothers and now was telling them to forget what happened and move on into the new and everything the future held for them.

This charge is the one Jesus has given us. Love one another and forgive so that we can live in peace. We are to forgive others and forget. The past cannot be changed.

Joseph is alive and well.

Genesis 45:26-28; 46:1-4 They told him, "Joseph is still alive! In fact, he is ruler of all Egypt." Jacob was stunned; he did not believe them. But when they told him everything Joseph had said to them, and when he saw the carts Joseph had sent to carry him back, the spirit of their father Jacob revived. And Israel said, "I'm convinced! My son Joseph is still alive. I will go and see him before I die."1 So Israel set out with all that was his, and when he reached Beersheba, he offered sacrifices to the God of his father Isaac. And God spoke to Israel in a vision at night and said, "Jacob! Jacob!" "Here I am," he replied. "I am God, the God of your father," he said. "Do not be afraid to go down to Egypt, for I will make you into a great nation there. I will go down to Egypt with you, and I will surely bring you back again. And Joseph's own hand will close your eyes."

Genesis 46:29 Joseph had his chariot made ready and went to Goshen to meet his father Israel. As soon as Joseph appeared before him, he threw his arms around his father and wept for a long time.

What an awesome day. Can you imagine the tears of joy and all they had to talk about? When the brothers tell the father the whole story, notice that he is not angry with the brothers for what they did. He is excited at what God has done.

I have seen God do this in so many families, mine included. Right at this moment as I am writing this book I am witnessing God doing this again in another family that was broken and full of hate. A daughter that could not forgive her mother and a family that was so disjointed has now been healed and made whole. I love watching God put all the pieces together, like only He can do.

This is a great example of God's plan of redemption in the lives of His people.

Chapter Nine

Pain an Unwelcome Stranger

My own life started to improve as I turned fifteen. I moved away from where I was living. I had found employment and a small granny flat at the back of a policeman's house. At last it seemed that my life was normal.

I had met some good people and started dating a great guy who really did love me, as much as you can at fifteen years old. He wanted to be with me and we had great times together. It was a season of fun, love, laughter and joy. Life seemed so good for the first time and I felt at peace.

We dated for about a year then both decided we were too young to be so serious and neither of us were ready for anything more. We decided at this stage of our lives just to be friends. He was possibly the first true friend that I had ever had. We remained really close friends and caught up with each other regularly. We both thought sometime in the future we would get back together.

Even though it was a little hard to let go, it felt right. I was starting to feel good about myself but I was not ready to settle down or be in a serious relationship.

Being loved that year brought a new confidence and happiness into my life and finally I could see a light at the end of what seemed a very dark, long tunnel. I had formed some good friendships and the next few months were just about having fun. It was the disco era and I loved dancing.

My friends and I would go to all night discos until 5am, head home for a shower and a change of clothes, then head straight to work. I never drank much, so I was never too 'hung over' to make it to work. Dancing seemed to energise me. I even won a dancing competition, this was my new passion. I enjoyed work and the freedom of having my own money and being self-sufficient. We never had much as kids and now I could buy nice things.

At work I met a girl that was very sad and broken, her life was so messed-up and I felt sorry for her. I could empathise with all she was going through. She had got herself into a bad relationship and needed help. I knew what it was like to be in great need, so I asked her to move in with me. This turned out to be a very bad decision on my part.

Unfortunately, she had some unhealthy friends and that is when I met my next boyfriend. I fell for the wrong guy and was now entangled and influenced by the wrong friends. He was fine when he was away from his friends, but they had a hold on his life and he was influenced by them.

Why couldn't I meet someone normal, why was I attracted to this type of person, and why were they so attracted to me?

I now know that when you are broken and not healed, it is like having an open wound. When left untreated, flies are attracted to it. In my case, the wrong type of guys. Eventually the wound becomes infected. Even worse, if it stays unhealed it eventually becomes gangrenous and has to be cut off leaving you impaired for life.

We dated and I found that I really liked this guy. There seemed to be a real attraction to him, I wanted to be with him, but not embrace his lifestyle or friends. I knew on the inside of me that this relationship was not good but when I was with him life seemed great. I guess the feeling of being loved once again ruled my better judgment. To have someone really want you is always so attractive and feels great when all you have known is rejection and felt so unloved and used. I always thought I was never good enough to be loved for who I am and now to have someone else wanting me and loving me was overwhelming. You think you can change them or the love you have will eventually break them from the bad influences in their life.

My life at this point took on a new twist that was again only going to end in heartache. I was sixteen and found myself pregnant. I was so excited and it seemed that life was going to be good for me. Was this my happily ever after, my fairytale come true? We could get married. I dreamed about us being together, one happy little family. I could love and be loved.

As the weeks went by my boyfriend began to become disinterested with me and our baby. His visits became less and less. The loneliness started to return but I was so excited about the baby.

Somehow when you feel so unloved the thought of a new life is exciting. Now I would have someone to love and a child to love me. Those were my thoughts on the situation. I always wanted to be a mother. This wasn't quite the dream. But nevertheless, a baby was exciting to me.

When you are as broken and as young as I was the perspective you have on life is often distorted. It is like looking at a serious situation through rose tinted glasses. I had no idea what this entailed. The responsibility, where the provision would come from... I hadn't even given it a thought. I guess inside of me I was always hoping for the fairy-tale of us being together.

It was around ten weeks into my pregnancy that I was woken one night with severe pain and heavy bleeding.

I was so scared and had no idea what was happening to me. I asked the girl I was staying with to drive me to hospital and call my boyfriend and tell him where I was.

After what seemed hours of pain and bleeding, they told me I had miscarried my baby and would need surgery the next day. My boyfriend never turned up, he never came. Again I was on my own and heartbroken. I was in total denial of what had happened to me. I was scared, alone and full of loss and grief. It felt that night that every bit of pain from the past was here with me again. An unwelcome stranger I knew so well. How did this happen? How was I at this point of pain again? It felt more painful than before and I felt so abandoned and on my own.

I had to sleep in a hospital gown as I had taken nothing with me to hospital and I had no one I could contact. There was a sweet old lady in the bed next to me, who I guess could hear me crying in my distress and realised that I had nobody coming to visit me. She asked her family to buy me a toothbrush, hairbrush and some toiletries.

I believe this was God looking after me, He was still there watching over me and waiting for me to reach out to Him.

Here I was broken, but in a different way. I knew this guy and his friends were not good for me and I needed to move away so I wouldn't be drawn back into a relationship with him. Once again I needed to run and make a new start. This time I was going far away where no one could find me.

My Mother lived in Queensland with her second husband. I packed up and moved there, as far away as I could possibly go. I hadn't lived with my Mother for many years. Mum and Dad were two broken people when they met and had three children before they were twenty one. They were unable to be together, they just had too much 'stuff'. They were both hurt and unhappy. Our childhood was very sad and dysfunctional. I had not lived with Mum for many years, so going to live with her now was a big step for me.

Mum was the happiest I had seen her in all of my life. My younger brother was also at home living with her and her second husband. I guess for her, it was the first time her life had any sense of normality or peace about it. She was excited that I had come home to live. I know that she has always loved me the best way she knew how, but unfortunately the measure of love that she had was small as she had not known love herself.

I did not understand this until much later in my life when God came through for me and healed me. I couldn't understand how a mother could leave her children. I thought she didn't love us. But she had loved us with all that she had. Life had dealt all my family some very unfair and hard things, as it does for so many people. It is a generational pattern that keeps repeating until someone steps up and reaches out to God to bring change that breaks the cycle.

Chapter Ten

Breaking The Cycle

I have seen God's plan of redemption in my own life. Once I called on Him and acknowledged him things began to change and turn around.

While I was living in Queensland, I was unhappy and didn't have any friends and my natural instinct was to return to where I had come from. I was bored and the highlight of the week was to go and watch my step-father play football and socialise at the club afterwards. I did not enjoy going, but it was better than staying at home.

One particular Saturday I was sitting and talking to a friend in the grandstand at the football and this guy kept staring at me and smiling. It was a little unnerving and I thought he was strange. At the end of the football game and after he had consumed several beers, he came across and asked me if I was going back to the club afterwards. My mother stepped in and said, "Yes, but not with you".

Upon returning to the clubhouse, I found this guy asleep in a chair. I was quite relieved as one of the girls told me he had a crush on me, but he was living with a girl and had been engaged three times. I knew at once that I definitely did not need this man in my life. I had just lost a baby and had recently come out of a bad relationship. This guy was trouble with a capital 'T'.

About half an hour later he woke and came over to me, asking me to go out with him. The rest of the night he kept calling me the name of the girl he was living with. I tried hard all night to get rid of him, but everywhere I went there he was.

My Mum was having some friends back to her house and thought that we were getting on well together, so she invited him back as well. My Mum wanted me to stay in Brisbane with her but she knew I was missing my friends. Her solution to the problem was to try and help me make new friends. He was very willing to accept the invitation, but I was not at all keen on the idea.

As he had drunk a lot of beer and lived a distance away, my mother offered him my brother's room for the night. All I wanted was to be rid of him. I was in dread of having to see him the next morning but I knew that he had to be at work at 11 am so he would soon be leaving, never to be seen again... or so I thought.

It was my brother's birthday and we were all going to the Coast for lunch to celebrate. I could not believe what happened next. My mother does the unthinkable and asks this guy to come with us. You guessed it, he accepts! Now I am stuck with him for another day.

Amazing as it may seem, when he was sober he was funny, nice, and enjoyable to be around. We had a good day together but I was aware that there were many obstacles in the way and I didn't need any more complications in my life. I didn't need to get involved with another guy who was not right for me. As it turned out he had only been engaged once but he was living with someone. That in itself was too much for me to handle so I spent the whole day telling him I would not go out with him.

But something changed within me. We had a great day and he took me on a walk up to a lighthouse. It was beautiful, on top of a hill overlooking the ocean. It was the most beautiful place I had ever been. I must admit, I hadn't been many places in my short life. It was raining lightly and on the way up he had stopped and picked a flower for me. On reaching the top he hugged and kissed me, and with that, I was gone.

This man is now my wonderful husband Greg, my Prince Charming to whom I have been married to for thirty-six years. Now don't get me wrong. It was a tough road like Leah, Tamar, Judah, Joseph and Jacob, to get to where we are today.

Eighteen months after we met, we married. But once again you have two broken people coming together with messed-up pasts. My husband was a heavy drinker. He loved to party and lived for his mates.

It was fun in the beginning because we were together and loved each other. Soon after we were married I found out I was expecting our first baby. I was eighteen and my husband was twenty-three. We were both excited about becoming parents, but we hadn't planned on having children for at least five years.

I was settling into becoming a mother and being family-orientated but my husband was still drinking every night and partying all weekend. His main things in life were his mates, football and cricket. I would go every week to the football even though I was very pregnant, sit all day on very uncomfortable seats, and then sit at the clubhouse while he drank and partied.

Most weeks I would go home alone and later get a phone call, somewhere between 3am to 5am asking me to come and pick him up from some party. Greg was often so drunk that he had no idea where he was and it would take me ages trying to get someone on the phone who knew where they were.

The night our beautiful baby was born Greg went out to celebrate with his mates. He got so drunk that he didn't make it to see us at all the next day. I was recovering from a caesarean section and being a new mum was very emotional and I was in a lot of pain. I needed him but he wasn't there for me. I started to worry and ask if he was alright. Was he in a car crash? There were no mobile phones in those days and I was barely sleeping worrying about him.

Greg arrived the next day, very sorry as always after that he had been drinking. Greg loved me but he also loved his mates and the drink. I was angry and hurt. He had let me down once again but I pushed it aside and got on with life.

I had become pretty good at just getting on with life after all the hurt. Disappointment was part of my life, a familiar friend. What I hadn't realised was that disappointment affects you, every hit has an effect. We start life with a pumping red heart full of love and joy. Every hit we get makes a black spot on our heart. While there are more red spots than black, you are fine and can seem to function. When life goes on and spots are unhealed, the red part of the heart gets smaller and smaller. Now ¾ of the heart is made up of black spots and ¼ red. No longer can you ignore the hurt and pain because you lose your love, joy and peace.

Often you become hard-hearted, cynical, jealous, and basically an unhappy person. Not much fun to be around. You don't know why you react the way you do. You don't want to be like this but the heart is the main organ of the body, it controls everything. Once we start to lose life everything begins to shut down. This was beginning to happen to me. I didn't feel like I used to feel. I wasn't as carefree as I use to be. I felt numb. I was just functioning and I was beginning to wonder what life was all about. I was starting to think about God and life. The hand of God was beginning to move in our family.

Greg's parents had a very difficult, hard life. Greg's father was also a heavy drinker and had put his family through a lot. Greg's mum had given up on him and their marriage. They were so desperate that when a friend asked them if they had ever tried God, they surrendered their lives to God and He turned them around.

At the time we were living in a flat downstairs in their home and they would often ask us to come to church on Sunday mornings. Greg was normally hung over on Sunday mornings so we always made an excuse not to go. One Sunday we agreed to go to a special service that night. I was excited as I had seen the change in his parents. I knew there was a God but had not experienced Him like Greg's parents had. Greg went out to his normal drinking session on the Sunday with his mates and upon returning home late in the afternoon told me he didn't want to go.

I was annoyed and angry with him and I had to tell his parents we would not be coming to church. I was so disappointed I packed up our six-week-old baby and decided to go out for the night. As I drove I was thinking "who can I visit, what can I do?" I had really wanted to go to church but the service was about to start and I had no idea how to get there.

I cried out to God and said, "If you are real, help me get to this church". Much to my amazement, I drove straight to the church without taking one wrong turn. This was my first miracle. I hadn't been living in Brisbane long and only had my driving licence for one year. I didn't know the area we were living very well. This church was in a part of Brisbane that I had never been to.

I don't remember any of the service, but I know when the invitation came to open my life to God and allow Him to come in. I was the first person at the front of that church. It was the most life-changing, powerful day of my life.

When I returned home later that night Greg says the moment I came through the door, even in his drunken state, he knew there was something different about me. He asked, "Where have you been, and what have you done?" When I told him, he replied "I want that for my life too".

Next Sunday we both went along to church with his sister. They both went forward when the invitation was given to receive Jesus into their lives. At the end of the service the three of us were baptised in water and came up out of the water filled with the Spirit of God.

What a life-changing day. From then on everything changed for us. But it hasn't been an easy road. There has been a lot of hard work, faith, and pushing through the many barriers.

God had to heal us from all the brokenness, generational habits, bad traits and so many other things. But just like Leah, Tamar, Jacob and Judah, when someone steps up and allows God into their lives, the results are amazing.

So often we look for quick results and quick fixes, but it takes time. Quick fixes are short term. God had to dismantle us and build a new foundation in our lives. We had to be open and willing and trust Him, believing that He knew what was best for us. We had to walk through the fires and be willing to go through the floods, but God was with us every step of the way.

Chapter Eleven

Happily Ever After, Generational Blessing

What I see now after thirty-six years is the breaking of generational patterns. I was headed for the same heartache as my previous generation but through God and our love for each other we were willing to do the 'hard yards' and stand in the gap.

We prayed that our children and our children's children would not know the brokenness, drunkenness, and abuse that had been in our generation. From this time on, our family will be blessed.

We have three beautiful children who have kept themselves pure until their marriage. They have all followed God's purpose for their lives and love God with all their hearts. They are loved, secure, and strong leaders. All three married equally incredible people with the same love for God. Our two daughters along with our amazing son-in-laws are Pastors of great churches. Our son and his beautiful wife serve in church. They are market-place ministers and both have a powerful call on their lives.

Greg and I have been in full time ministry for twenty-four years and are blessed to travel the world teaching, training, and empowering lives. It has been an incredible journey.

He took a little girl who felt she was nobody's child and turned her life around. I was His child and He had a plan for me. The little girl who hadn't been to many places or had much in life now has abundance and has visited places she would never have dreamed of. My life is blessed and is a miracle and testimony to the power of God. I found my Prince Charming and God gave me my happily ever after.

God has been so good to us. I now see in our lives, just as in the word of God, that it doesn't matter how messed-up you family is, God can make it good and turn around a whole generation.

We have five beautiful grandchildren. I look at them and know they will do amazing things because we have a generation that is blessed. It just keeps getting stronger. So many of our family members have given their lives over to God as they have seen the difference He has made in our lives and family.

We were broken, messed-up and full of the things that plagued Jacob, Leah, Judah and Tamar, but God had a plan for them and God has a plan for us. He has a dream for each and every one of us. He predestined you and knew you before you were formed in your mother's womb. He is waiting for you to call upon Him.

It was the best call we ever made and it has an eternal affect.

Jeremiah 29:11-13 11 For I know the plans I have for you," declares the LORD, "plans to prosper you and not to harm you, plans to give you hope and a future. Then you will call upon me and come and pray to me, and I will listen to you. You will seek me and find me when you seek me with all your heart.

There is no mountain too high, no valley too deep, or mess too big that God cannot fix. God will lift you up out of your mess and turn your family around, but we must first put out our hand to Him. His hand is already there. It is so easy, one simple decision and your life is changed forever.

John 3:16-18 This is how much God loved the world; He gave his Son, his one and only son. And this is why: so that no one need be destroyed by believing in Him, anyone can have a whole and lasting life. Message Bible.

Romans 10:9 "If you declare with your mouth, Jesus is Lord," and believe in your heart that God raised him from the dead, you will be saved.

Matthew 10:32 Therefore whoever confesses Me before men, him I will also confess before my Father who is in heaven. NKJ

There are four steps that you need to take:

1. Repent for your sins, tell God you are sorry for what you have done and receive His forgiveness.
2. Believe in your heart that He died and rose again.
3. Confess with your mouth that He is now Lord of your life.
4. Go and tell someone and find a church and people who will support your decision to follow Christ.

CPSIA information can be obtained
at www.ICGtesting.com
Printed in the USA
FFOW01n0619250318
45949209-46846FF

9 781634 929653